Letter to Patience
John Haynes

seren

Seren is the book imprint of
Poetry Wales Press Ltd
57 Nolton Street, Bridgend, Wales, CF31 3AE
www.seren-books.com

ISBN 1-85411-412-3

A CIP record for this title is available from the British Library.

The publisher acknowledges the financial assistance
of the Welsh Books Council.

Printed in Hoefler Text by Bell & Bain, Glasgow.

PREFACE

Patience' Parlour is a small mud-walled bar in Northern Nigeria in the village of Samaru. Samaru's geometrical grid of dirt streets, originally laid by the British, provides a market, a mosque, churches, beer parlours and houses for junior staff at Ahmadu Bello University across the main road. Beyond and around it is farmland where guinea corn, maize and groundnuts are grown, and you see white humped-backed cattle watched and mouth-clicked at by a ten year old boy with a stick and a raffia hat.

At the time the poem is set, Patience herself is thirtyish and has lived in Samaru for some fifteen years, first as a student, then as a lecturer in Politics at the university, a job which she has given up partly because of junta pressures on radical academics and journalists, and partly on principle: it seems to her that political education has to happen elsewhere.

Though her origins are far south in Benin City, she has got used to Samaru and it has become home, despite the periodically whipped up local prejudice against non-Hausas and non-Muslims. The bar was attacked by the so-called *Ayatollahs* in 1988, her fridge and tables wrecked, her bottles smashed in the streets, and it would have been torched had it not backed onto the property of her well-to-do Hausa landlord.

If you leave the university by the back gates, cross the road to the trestle table stalls on the other side, go alongside the market, pass the mosque, and then follow the dirt streets with their mud houses, cinemas, food hotels, stalls of kebab griddles, you get to her bar with its coloured bulbs on a board outside. It is adapted from a traditional compound with a large patio around which are set other rooms, built as separate structures. The largest, which you come into from the street entrance, forms the inside bar, essential during rainy season.

5

Other rooms are used for a kitchen, store room with two fridges full of bottled lager, and there is a traditional shower/toilet into which, at night, you take your candle and smear/stick it on the wall. There is electricity, but not throughout, and the main lighting comes from hurricane lamps which don't go out in the frequent power cuts. The patio is filled with rough plank tables, benches and chairs. There is a well at one end, and further rooms where Patience's teenage daughters live.

In the 1980s *Patience' Parlour* was a watering hole for radicals from the university. But the drinkers, who form the 'cast' of the poem, come from all walks of life (see Notes).

The letter is set in 1993 at a time of unrest just before President Babangina was to annul the apparently perfectly fair elections which were won by Mashood Abiola who, although very far from being a man of the people, was both a Muslim and a Southerner, and so promised to be a truly national choice. Hence the unity of the nation was felt to be threatened and ethnic differences came to the fore.

The Letter Writer writes from England to which he has returned with his Nigerian wife and children to nurse his dying father. His parents had been musicians in music hall, pantomime and summer shows, his maternal grandfather a Cornish tin mining engineer who, after the collapse of the industry in 1860, went to the gold mines of South Africa, where the Letter Writer's mother was born.

The poem as a whole represents the hours from about 1 a.m. when the Letter Writer starts writing, to first light when he leaves off.

Brief explanations of places, people and events are given in the Notes at the end of the book.

When we say "Time" we mean ourselves.
Most abstractions are simply our pseudonyms.
It is superfluous to say "Time is scytheless and
toothless." We know it. We are time.

– C P Cavafi

For nimble thought can jump both sea and land
As soon as think the place where he would be.
But, ah! thought kills me that I am not thought

– William Shakespeare, Sonnet XLIV

...the word 'I' does not have a central place in
grammar, but is a word like any other.

– Ludwig Wittgenstein

LETTER TO PATIENCE

I

The Cottage, 70 Padnell Road, Cowplain,
Hants, England, 5th May, 1993.
Patience – as I begin this yet again

now everyone's asleep, the BBC
World Service News is on its perfect line
along that line once ruled invisibly

across the globe to where that watch of mine
ticks on the inside of your wrist. Mosquito-
thin red second hand, you can refine

us to a single *now* jerk *now*, zero
meridian, across this black glass sky
with its own grid of panes and stars, and slow

pulse winking, like some tropical firefly
inching away. It could be taking this
tomorrow where time's real rules still apply:

sea, desert, savannah, airport, post office
with its dates and stamps, and then the bare
tyres bumping over dust with this homesickness

or something like it, turning *here* to *there,*
and *now* to *then,* except that now, before
even the words I'm even half aware

I want to mean form in my mouth, as sure
and speechless as the ink itself, I hear
you hearing them, as if I'm some folk-lore

style ghost that needs no corridor to steer
through space or time, as if the see-through head
reflected like a kite on this sky near

us both, might bring these words not yet quite said.
My ghost, the paper soul of me that slips
away, leaving its cell of bone for dead

awhile, here, two o'clock, the first few pips
before the news again on BBC,
and hands typing by touch. No, fingertips.

II

Go little spirit, then, and I can see
the candles wobbling on those stalls outside
the campus gate, the piles of *Ambi, Maggi*

Cubes, tea bags, the mosquito coils, the dried
crayfish in twists of polythene, the tray
with Saddam Hussein's face on it, the fried

yam clicking in its oil as Mamma Ture
bends village style down to her wide black pans,
her toes spread out, her bum hoisted, her grey

logs nothing now but beards, the Peak Milk cans
with tugging wicks of cotton wool, the flare
of charcoal from the suya sellers' fans,

house-fronts swaying in fumes, through pepper air
the coloured lightbulbs rattling on your bar
making the tree in front as vague as hair,

the drain wrinkly with rainbows, the car
sunk to its rusted wheel hubs in the dust,
door jamb, handbills for *Double Crown* and *Star,*

thin slits of light, reggae, voices, a gust
of laughter. As if I could make that bit
of threadbare cloth push back, as if I just

might feel the wall resist my palm, its grit
just shifting first, then underneath, the glow
of that sun right down in the mud of it....

III

As if it's all there still, a road, a row
of houses with the horns and plasticine-
like joins of walls, as if the radio

is wrong, or here has not been touched, there's been
no rioting, no churches have been torched,
no beer tipped in the gutters, no *shebeen*

(as they called it) left with its roofbeams scorched
and smoking among broken chairs and glass,
no *women from Hollywood Clob* debauched

and stoned for harlots, as if men with scars
and home made bandages had not crammed Kano
junction struggling into buses, cars

taxies, mammy wagons. I don't know
where to address this to you in Benin
City, Patience. I'll send it care of Joe

at the department, if in fact Joe's in
the office still – yes, I know, for some clerk
to crumple up and lob towards the bin

with all the others which have this postmark
and nothing in them but the words? And yet,
it's just words, isn't it – the helpless stark

unlikelihood that they will ever get
to you – that makes me weigh the empty air
and shape of each. As if to hedge a bet.

IV

My daughter's new Bob Marley hair
beads click each time she moves her head, asleep
against the broad arm of the easy chair.

This was their Music Room and we still keep
the Francis Day & Hunter songs in place
along the shelves. My childhood tunes are deep

into the walls and floorboards here, their base
between pantos and summer shows. They look
from sterling silver frames into the space

from which applause should come. Outside, a hook
and chain suspends *The Cottage* in the ye
old letters of a children's story book.

Sometimes we act them out at bedtime, Ratty,
Badger, Mole, hallooing *Hey you fellows*
from the garden in their good chap RP,

those upright beasts dressed in Victorian clothes
that make you laugh. Lara's got a green
felt Mr Toad. His humbug eyes don't close

for all she hugs, just blink back as this screen
blinks, towards shelves of *Tarzan*, paper music,
Porter, Gershwin, Berlin, Kern – Dad's has-been

ancestors whose *Darkies* clinked an Afrik
banjo gut as if their fingering
might just retune the sun's own rays to pick

out human intervals along a string
and fret, just like the ancient profs, with skin
almost as dark, who made the numbers sing

for young Pythagoras when he sat in
their bars – like yours – drunk to the selfless essence
floating from his body like a djin

in timeless *now*. Exactly now, Patience,
I too want to make all Africa narrow
to a mud walled bar. There's arrogance.

V

As I think the thought of it a shadow
tumbler prints the creosoted top
of a plank table with those little hollow

ovals like a spider's web. A drop
of fat bursts into charcoal smoke that lifts
in rags across the voices, reggae, pop

of bottle tops, recalling, as it drifts
and thins away, some textbook entropy
stopped in the photograph's siftings and shifts

here, far off, at a screen, in memory
where there's no time, only a sense of sight
that's always there behind the eyes exactly

now, your stiff headtie, your nyash wrapped tight
in *george* as always, the wet bottles gleam-
ing in your elbows, now as every night

both there and here, both real and in the dream
in which your ghost is standing there again
unknown to you, as in a spotlight beam,

caught in the slime and wrinkles of a brain
that isn't yours, and synapse pulse and node
dissolve you Star Trek style into a rain

then in its other time and space reload
each cliché over cliché, till it's you,
again, half juju and half genome code,

now moving through the bar with *esewu*
in little wooden tubs. The gobbets shine
and steam and wobble in the soup, grey-blue

goat lip, goat nostril, goat eye, ear. "Fine-fine
na you go mek book, John, wid dis kain brain
for dey insai." And yet it isn't mine,

is it, nor yours, this picture from a chain
of nerves that spreads and spreads out of my head
like pins and needles, that I can't contain?

VI

"The bar is what you're going to miss," you said,
"not me," but that's wrong isn't it, to draw
lines around people (even if they're dead),

as if I'd miss the place you live in more
than you, when there's no line between at all
and that's something that *you* kept saying, *your*

philosophy, the sense of floor, mud wall,
dust road as who we are, the kites' long cry
at harmattan, the beggar's rhythmic call

outside Alhaji Kowa's store, this *I*
that floats and enters you from just as far
as ever, dear one, shapeless as the sigh

that lifts out of your mouth, out of the bar,
out of the rusted corrugated zinc
and mixes with some wailing armoured car

out on the road, and then the first tink-tink
of birds, the cockerel's call, none of it you,
except that when I think of it I think

it is and not the old *femme noire, femme nue*
'Afrique', no, something shared in spite of skin
colour, and Lugard's maxim gun, or *through*

just those, is it? I think so, what we're in,
as what we are. And so I'm writing this
Magana Jari Ce, am I, to spin

you into words? A spell, a selfishness
to try and keep you there, or rather here,
closing my eyes with lust to see, miss

you, sharper – no, the bar, music, the beer?
Or it's an elegy for someone dead
for all I know, for all I fear to fear.

VII

After my mother died I went to Red-
stone Hill, swooshing the leaves up through the same
woods I'd walked as a boy towards that bed

in that cold dormitory where she came
more real than in real life inside a cone
of spotlight, touched the steel tubing his name

was labelled to, and sang to him alone,
the blubby baby newbug with the damnfool
stick-out ears. Patience, I have to own

up to my empire making boarding school,
of course I do. It educated me....
So when she died, I went, stood by the pool,

looked at the brownish water in the vee
made by the concrete – cracked now, weeds in it –
remembering how clean it used to be

for swimming sports, and how we'd dive and split
its insubstantial glitter on the gun
then gag for lack of breath. There's still some grit

left from the drive. The trees still keep the sun
off where the forecourt circle was. Mayflies,
blackberries, nettles, stone steps overrun

with ground ivy. Vandals from the high rise
set fire to it. The walls are gone. There's ash
like porridge on my boots. Behind it lies

the green air of the jungle and this hash
of years of leaves, and old planks from the shed
where Tarzan used to come to see his cache

of human things: his father's knife, the bed
on which his own Mum's bones still lay, the cot
with that small skeleton put there instead

of him, the changeling of an ape. The plot
writ in his genes – part folktale, part Lamarck,
part racist pulp – returned him here. The blot

of his baby fingerprint. *Noah's Ark*
with his true name in it, from which impos-
sibly, he'd work out every bug-like mark

he found again and then again across
the page, not realising that he should,
dead as they were, speak them aloud. The loss

of everything except the skin he stood
inside was what he found. It brought him back
to his true Englishness, since there he could,

strange pale thing that he was, turn all his lack
of mother love to strength, and run and fight
and swim and jump and climb and track. And track.

VIII

Tracks, traces, tokens, trophies. Jungle light
becomes museum glass, their backs and arms
and necks able to twist like that in spite

of nature since they *are* just art. No qualms
of conscience, no shame, and no characters.
Only their shapes are human. Gods of farms?

Ancestors? Souls changed in the camera's
white prejudice again, this time to coffee
table ones some careful editor's

assigned a tribe and a geography.
And there they shag, mouths yawning out for it,
all poles and holes, no longer piously,

nor fertile, but as we say, *explicit.*
Merchandise, that should have been sent back
like all the reproductions we exhibit

in the theatre of the brain. I'll pack
and freight them back to *you,* shall I? The not-
returnable, not-mine, not-me, rucksack

which the sweating pilgrim bears, so hot
for far off love... Shall I? Your hand, your eye,
your mouth – item by item, lot by lot?

IX

Fertility, the primitive: how high
heels of space alloy, and tights smooth as sand
define the definition of a thigh.

X

"Woman – is a Dark Continent", his hand
guiding a golden nib, wrote Sigmund Freud,
professor of the soul: that hinterland

you have to penetrate and find your void
to people with desire, the *theatre*
(Mercator's word for map) where anthropoid

and can-can dancer grunt-whirl-laugh together
among humming birds, melting in time,
bristly groin to delicate suspender,

the *Empire* with red velvet seats and lime
light and the legs and Rule Britannia bit,
which are, I know, what make the paradigm

of the exotic body I inherit –
Mum in panto with high boots as Jack,
Mum singing *Bill* at Margate where I sit

and watch the spotlight in my head far back
here in the dark. Pale Pierrots. Concert party,
minstrels with white faces made-up black.

A chorus girl's abstract geometry
bestrides his oceans with her fishnet thighs,
our Circumnavigator constantly

invoking his fixed stars. Which are her eyes.
They mark his longitudes whatever voo-
doo dancer takes her place in her disguise

of flesh. None of these ghosts, I know, is *you,*
Patience, swerving round chairbacks in a bar,
round tables, shoulders, swooping plate of stew

and rice and plantain in each hand, or *Star*
beers flat down, to fizz cold smoking open....
Although, of course, of course, of course, they are,

aren't they? And that's our depth, just as this token
of the empty English pronoun I
pronounce is the same pronoun that is spoken

to the dead, or fills a singer's cry,
or was once substituted for the name
some barque of Injun gold was guided by.

XI

The times shown on our watches are the same.
Across the map those strangers drew a net
of pure Pythagorean lines to claim

time as their own, and hold it still, and set
the farthest places in the head at rest.
So in Hogg Robinson's you see the jet

routes on a tissue paper lampshade stressed
with latitudes and longitudes of wire
and numbered with the hours to East and West

from zero, where (almost) your cooking fire
keeps time with these computer clicks. This *now*
shrinks everything into its own empire.

So much for Einstein's boyhood dream of how
it might feel riding on a beam of light.
So much for looking at somebody's brow

to see how old they are, or at the height
the sun has curved above the roadside stand
you sit under and watch the tyre boys light

an acrid, drooling rubber flame that's fanned
with *Time Life* sporting Mrs Thatcher's face,
now staring from a wheel-rim in the sand

next to the railway track. Or for the place
at which the lines will reach infinity
and meet and vanish there. A kind of grace

in that, the way it seems the ordinary
earth touches the sky exactly where
your gaze is fixed. Kind of tautology.

The same platonic grid of square on square
marks out the shantytown, the roofs of rust
that passengers can point at from the air

since they are white, and punctual, and trust
in calendars and charts, since they can fly.
Below, the players' bare feet in the dust

move round the pingpong table. On the sky
their ball moves like a moon going to and fro
across the propped-up-books for net, and, eye

and hand fixed on its cosmic little O,
they crouch and swing and lunge with chip and tock
and tick as vapour trails widen their slow

motion time like smoke across the rock
music and shoulders in a township bar
and from the wrecked Beetle outside, a cock

muezzins with claws curled round a rusty spar,
"Na you don mek di blod I sing wit red,"
through gritty air to its alarm-clock star.

XII

We are time. Time's wheel, time's stone arrowhead,
time's timeless present tense, not now, not this,
not here, where no bare kids glitter like lead

next to a compound well, no bottles hiss,
tops tinkling down under the table planks,
no tumblers lift, no lips purse into "Bis-

simillahi!" here also to give thanks!
"Life's but a wayside farm," no singer sings
or looks up from the dust towards the ranks

of roofs, and stars, and washing-line strings:
"Life's but a wayside farm." No Sunday drunk
asleep straight upright in his chair, the wings

of his nose tensing, untensing, his chin sunk
solemn to his Zaria Rugby Club tie.
No Sani, foot caressed in palm, and chunk

of meat in cheek and intent specs from eye
to eye across the bottles' necks: the way
Saddam's been demonised, the way the spy

and torture boys come in from RSA,
Israel, the end of the USSR,
Third World helpless against the CIA

terrorists, bankers (pause) and bourgeois
so-called Marxist expatriates with sly
agendas – as you slide another Star

up to his wristwatch and mosquitoes fly
electron patterns round his ears with thin
high screams. "Whatever else you people try

to nit-pick history with, still Stalin
knew that to change a country you must kill
some people!" No honey coloured flame in

each lens fixing my gaze fixing a quill
of creosote, like one of those here on
the wall in this snap of you dressed to kill

in fetish length high heels with *love to John*
and thighs torpedoing from miniskirt.
Not you. In place of you: a glossy con.

The white man's magic can longer hurt.
See, there's the shadow of his head and arm
holding the instant flash that will convert

you into light transfixed on card. A charm,
a charm, nothing, a powerless powerful wish
to save someone I cannot save from harm?

XIII

Dressed to kill, to be killed, that is. A swish
of robes and bare soles over dust going through
the unlit township: I see them, the fetish

on the pendant round the neck, The True
Believers. And their *Allah Akbar* comes
in such small hours as these, when they renew

the holy bottle-smashing in the slums
built once for mission scholars to maintain
that Mandate with their copperplate and sums....

You brush the gently trickling sugar-grain
of glass across the porch. No table, chair,
or shelf unbroken. And they'll come again,

ragged *almajarai* as well, with bare
feet, silver heads, cans clanking in their queue
behind a dim Mercedes Benz. The air

turns sickly with fuel glip gloop glooping through
a plastic tube. The door splits open. "Fuck
you all, you Nazarenes!" There's Sa'idu,

your bar-boy, twelve years old, whose name means *luck*.
From where you're hiding underneath the bed
you watch him pick the oil lamp up to chuck.

"Just then," you said, "we were already dead,
yells, the crunches of an axe, a fall
of something big we couldn't see. Instead,

though, praise to God! – we heard Alhaji call
out "tsayan-ku – stop, all of you! Go back!" –
afraid the flames might reach his compound wall.

Next day, *as usual*, as it were, a sack
across his narrow shoulder, he comes in –
Sa'idu – standing there, big-grinning, crack-

ing knuckles, saying, "Madam, we get pickin
I beg: forgive me now", and kneels. "Today,
I tink I go wok well-well for kitchen

again, madam? Clean *all*, madam? Okay,
madam? Okay? Okay?" Who has done this?
you think, and looking at him, cannot say.

XIV

The gods sit in their rows of dark. They hiss.
They cup their hands around their mouths and bawl
advice, they know, however much they miss

the world, can't get through that see-through fourth wall,
however much they may become the play
and fill the players' emptiness of all

except the characters, the phrases they
find coming to their mouths as quick as lies
because a person's fate is what they say

it is, since here conviction's what denies
exactly by exactly rendering –
the script of what they slowly realise.

The flies billow up from the goat blood seeping
from the slugged door of the fridge. The rainbow
lizards cling against the mud wall, nodding

at a world they must make move to show
itself. Our camouflage is who we are.
Mimesis, mimicry. Our gazes blow

like angels along camera beams. The far
off ribs and chin-bones of the damned wait there
in close-up for our chair and cup of char,

shayi. Perhaps the gods in their despair,
and their disgust, look down and fantasise,
as at a melodrama, or some fair-

ground moral play, or tv news for eyes
and voice-over, as if seen in the head.
And even this, for all they agonise

and curse their sons' and daughters' being fed
by conquerors, still lets them empathise,
and, yes, takes off the edge of being dead.

XV

Here, nothing seems to be quite real. The flies
move on the baby's close-up cheek. The goals
burst from the faces of the fans. The eyes

of lemurs peer into our rooms like souls
beyond the screen. Now it's clown's noses on,
and bring the damned relief, and camera holes

right through the middles of their eyes. No non-
sense practicality, no nonsense food,
not conquest now. The conquerors have gone.

Into the very map's exactitude.
Earth measurers. And I can still now see
the chalk lines on a prepschool board, too crude,

I learnt, to touch the true geometry
which has no magnitude and cannot lie
and is, thought Socrates, just memory:

the backdoor step, Mum's washing line, the sky,
the grass, the scent of wallflowers, a home-
sickness as empty as the pronoun *I*.

XVI

Darkies, they *made a living* from. Jerome
Kern's, Gershwin's, Berlin's, my mum as Bess
on stage. But now this actual wooden comb:

he stares at it like someone in a *Guess
The Object* panel game. "It's from last night?
Afi brought Laraba down here to dress

her hair and watch *Show Boat* with you? All right?"
"A comb, that's all, Dad." *"Comb!?"* He can't recall,
of course, suddenly frightened with the light

snapped on. *"African* comb." "I di'n't' call."
"You did." *"Did* I?" And then again, "Wha's this?
Wha's this doin' here?" Rewind. Rewind. Paul

Robeson hauls dripping ropes and sings that *dis*
and *dem* kind Darkie lyric which the white
song makers wanted in that voice of his.

As if the ancestor within just might
be conjured up before the camera crew,
translated into technicolour light

by empathy and bulbs and cable. Through
which Kern himself was trying to understand
his own Old River Jordan's Time, a Jew

out of the pogroms of that Russian Band
Leader the windup ragtime phonogram
transformed from Czar to minstrel on the sand

at Cliftonville. There's Dad, black as the jam
jar golly wid de white lips at de keys.
COME ON AND HEAR! DE BESTEST BAND DAT AM!

When I was four maybe, his harmonies,
her voice downstairs rehearsing, and the song
like pins and needles in the floor would ease

me into sleep. And nothing of the wrong
that drove those Tin Pan Alley pioneers,
to Uncle Sam, to be safe there, belong

as belong could. Their tunes translated fears
I couldn't start to share into this thing
the tunes call love. When Mum did *Bill* real tears

would balance on her eyes. I watch her sing
as if to me, or hear a top note climb
out of the theatre roof towards a string

of bulbs above a carpark mesh where I'm
still waiting among coloured puddles. Julie's
song of common love and someone's crime

left in her blood. But what you cannot see's
one trace on Mum's (or Ava Gardner's) skin.
Nor on Dad's hands holding those harmonies

that Fats's bakelite *Ain't Misbehavin'*
fingers really hold. Maestro. Mastah.
"What's this thing doin' here, John? What's it doin'...?"

XVII

It's seven years, but there he is, Vatsa,
the baby cheeks crumpling the national scars
up underneath the eyes, the grin, RASTA

across the T-shirt behind rows of *Stars*,
still going on about his great city
"where literature and art," – now his cigar's

scrawling red lines across the air, – "will be
more celebrated, *and more sponsored*, than..."
for all the doom in his economy

ransacked by gamblers and some World Bank plan.
Days later he was shot as so-called *coup
plotter*, and Babangida put a ban

to stop us mourning him in print. All through
he still believed that IBB would send
an order to release him, once the due

tough gesture had been made – his townsman, friend,
comrade, and Sandhurst classmate. And this hope
M kept, quick-eyes-shut-nodding, to the end,

when they had wrapped him round with that white rope,
against a Shell Nigeria oil drum,
yelling across the beach, "Think I can't cope

up unblindfolded with you shower of dumb
small boys?" His shot guts came out at the back
turned blurry in the photos that would come

to market stalls, two naira for a pack
of six. I can't quite say I was his friend,
or that I liked his poems much. They lack,

for all the *Africanism* he'd defend
at seminars – let's say – a powerlessness.
He slightly frightened me. But in the end

it's not his power, his poems, his friendliness,
the Writers' Village (which before he died
he had already signposted) – but this,

I keep remembering: him as our guide
one ANA conference, swinging from the thong
in the coach roof and waving round his hide

and iroko swagger stick towards long
avenues of building sites. Then Hotel
Sheraton Abuja, clumping along

planks, and down steps into a sudden smell
of new wallpaper, thick carpet, a glow
of subtle lighting. Over this, the *shell*

of all else, the whole edifice, would grow,
a kind of super de luxe dungeon, right
down at the base of it: *The Casino Afro*.

XVIII

The madman, *he* directs the traffic: bright
black polished shoes and black suit like a pastor,
the bowler hat, the brolly. Now the white

flourish of the gloves, the fists spinning faster,
slower. Now the tickling little eye-
brow-lifted friendly come-ons, now master

of it all with STOP, the flat hand high,
the lower lip pushed down the chin – as taxi,
car, mammy wagon, bus, all just surge by,

all those windscreens of grins he doesn't see,
still whirling on his polished heel, the slick
gloves whizzing round again. Authority,

he ride it like a *bori*, with the magic
trick of staring from his own clear sight
unseen. The madman, *he* directs the traffic.

XIX

Calabar. Five years ago today. "Light
like pencil lead," I'd noted down. "Canoes
that once ferried the damned towards the white

sailed Christian ships out in the bay (*Na whose
soul you go catch for chain?*) with mounds of sand
for building sites upstream (*Whose you go lose?*).

The far bank: zigzag palm tree spikes that stand
black on the sky just like the ones you find
in Tarzan comic strips. Now this guy's hand

lifts in greeting, the ferry steamer's blind
clink-ink coming through mist, you couldn't say
how far away, or old, or real, outlined

with its own shadow. In flip-flops and grey
French suit, he comes, stepping over the hens
in nets, bags, nods at my pad: *You are may-*

be an inspector of some kind? but then's
already turned away, shouting in Efik
back to where the steamer's come in, men's

robes parachuting as they jump, the thick
pier logs bumping at the half-tyres, the crowd
cramming the plankways, and now the guy's quick

flip-flops slapping off again, calling loud
towards navvies who turn silver chests slowly
next to bales and funnel and swaying cloud."

I wrote it down. A place of slaves. A quay
of ghosts. A slop and smack of waves. A scrawl.
Inspector of some kind, maybe? Maybe.

XX

I keep seeing that blackened car, the pall
of smoke, the lake like silverfoil, again
the blood, the glass, the roadside sand, the small

long, high up cries of kites, then from the plane
tree tops with shadows, toy Heathrow, her gaze –
now all that's left of his – becoming train

and taxi, shopfront, wet pavement, the blaze
of hotel glass, wallpapered dark, all night
a radio that plays and talks and plays

half dream half memory in which the bright
splinters of his glasses come gently one
by one from his dead cheek as if they might

still hurt. The mind pretends, as it has done
always, and there aren't edges to their bodies
yet, and still the moments when they'd come

go back each time through all the memories
they ever had of touching anything,
her present tense of handprints, indices,

signs, scratches, vibrations that she can bring
back now, her ideology of clues
in evidence of what makes it all cling

together as a dung beetle's spit glues
a loved world round itself, but at no stage
along the line of it now. She can choose:

this then, that other now. He has no age
beyond the timeless tense time, now bizarre
in being mundane across the paper page

in which the narrative – *the blackened car,
the smoke,* their arbitrary names – turn back
into the few English phonemes there are.

XXI

Black Consciousness. *The Whiteman's soul is black.*
The shadow of his body is more native
to the Earth than he is, and treks back

through myths, through dreams to find that primitive
interior where just this fate was set
and there again that twin's exposed to live

or die, that *abiku* he's never met
who lives among the magic beasts in place
of him and who will teach him to forget

what I have conned by heart among a race
for whom the soul is like a clock, and wheel
enmeshed in wheel whirls round behind the face

and measures what it cannot reach or feel,
my Greenwich line, my longitude zero,
the centre of my globe, my common weal...

"Mistah John – he black! Still Mbulelo
grins across the tumblers out of nineteen
seventy-six, our child of Soweto

come home from exiled home to your shebeen
to hold our seven o'clock Booze Seminar
or eight-thirty-ish, or ten fifteen...

African time, Black Consciousness, "The star
on Che's beret," he starts, "there on the wall
above us, those blank grids of calendar...."

XXII

A myth of hope. A camouflage. The call
of hoopoes came out of his lips. The stream
was him, so was the tick and tocking fall

of rain. He was the leaves, the inner seam
of sun and chlorophyll from which his eye
evolved, his variation on a theme.

Someone had seen him in the market buy-
ing fish. Someone had seen him in the taxi
park, holding a bag, sunshades, tie-dye,

boot slamming, shouting touts, the dust. A tree,
a rag, a blackboard in the village. *Loot,*
spell it, spell *loot*, spell *looter*, feel them, see

the shape of them, the words, the rhymes, spell *shoot,*
like Gizo-gizo making loops unreel
out of his body. Write it: *rifle, boot,*

relocation. What else? It's you, the real.
It comes of saying it out loud. *You are,*
it is, they're doing this, say it, they steal,

the dam makers, oilmen, Barclays: com-pra-
dor. *Write it down.* His shadow slips between
our chair-backs in a mud-walled township bar

Or is it his? The girl's thighs gently seem
to swell under the table next to him.
She holds his simple blood. She holds the stream,

the leaves and twigs like camouflage denim,
the chlorophyll, the Ancestors who call
out jokes across that brilliance they swim....

XXIII

"An endless sense of love..." And now, yes, all
that he, Cabral, Fanon and others said
sounds unrealistic as the clichés fall

from *manjar janar's* patriotic head
filling your colour tv screen up. Same
speech, same coup, same uniform, same dead,

same mosques or churches going up in flame,
same throats being cut like goats in Samaru,
same *Go home!* half a lifetime since you came

and learnt the tongue you now hear cursing you.
Which *home* is that!? Each night the lamps reveal
the trickle at your temple bent to blue

barked cooking logs, the glint of steel high-heel
tips at the wrapper's hem, the shine-black lips,
gold earrings... Drink by drink and meal by meal

you tread your waiting times with careful hips.
Accounts and orders, the girls' high school fees,
the licence bribes, the breakages, the tips:

as if these rituals of coping, these
seconds linked to seconds without break,
answered the killing like a timeless frieze.

XXIV

It's us and London Scottish. For the sake
of Zazzau the Emir is pleased to send
three courtiers in robes to watch the make-

believe: attack, gain ground, break-through, defend.
An international. Lines ruled in grass,
and shirts with numbers on them. Real's pretend.

Abstract is violent. Timing his pass
through perfect space, Sunday sends Musa free
into the sudden din of hooting cars,

a bugle, drums, coke cans, and *eh-yeh-yeh yeeeeeeeee!*
of women's throats hitting the clouds from all
along the touchline. But the referee

won't have it. Scrum. The packs whumph in. Their ball,
the stand-off jinking past first Ahmadu
then Musa's dive, feeding inside, a maul,

then back to him again, his time, inch true,
calm, his brain slowed down, the silver kick
spins from his cultured boot. And Umaru

waiting as they close in on him, stoic
Hanwa farmer as he is, with no sign
of nerves or fear, now cornered in the thick

white right angle where goal line meets touch line
and cradling forth his arms towards the sky,
with all the breath he has, calls out: "Mine! Mine!"

XXV

Another ritual. I'm watching high
up with dark glasses in the Polo Park
and orange dust is lifting to the sky

and through it horses, turbans, the squark-squark
of long trumpets with pennants, spears. *Ya zo!*
He comes. The turban with the 'ears' that mark

his royal blood is swaying to and fro
inside the white lace curtained bower. He
who's to be made Emir. *Long Life,* elbow

bent to the dust, fist clenched, they cry, *Sarki!*
Sarki!, the timeless people, as horns squark
louder. Policemen with whips, headphoned tv

crews. Now sirens, outriders round the dark
green Merc, doors opening, salutes, the cheek
in profile as the anthem plays, the mark

of Sandhurst in the shadow of the peak,
Soja Gwabna looking at a small card:
I today appoint you... A sudden squeak

of mic and readjustment and the bard
rehearses lineage from Sultan Bello
through Attahiru, killed by the dog, Lugard,

down to this young man who blinks his slow
lashes listening, slips off a shoe, the song
describing *him* now, he whose heart is so

generous to us, so learned, the strong
bull elephant, the lion, but no hint
of it across his face, who's never wrong,

whose calmness comes from Allah with the glint
of holy spears, now bayonets on guard
across this grass fresh as a postcard print

after the Polo Club sprinklers. The bard,
not losing metre once, rises to praise
his Head of State in words that praised Lugard

before him, dog as he has been, his face
as pallid as a ghost's, the strange blue eyes,
the shorts, the long socks, the scout knife as always

clipped to his belt, the stiff salute through flies
and dust and din, old *Mai Gashin Baki,*
old *Him with the Moustache, The One Who Tries,*

and who could stand so long he probably
wore iron trousers, Grand Conquistador
of Sokoto, he whose artillery

turned Kano's mythic walls to nothing more
than flying puffs of sand, he who could vet
Allah's choice of Emir, and by what law,

decree what terms of reference be set
with his gold nib and iron guns. No need
of iron now. His eyes and cheeks are wet.

XXVI

"Our rubbish pits outlive us, John! The peed
on peel, the terra cotta turds down there
in Patience' soakaway. Look hard, now, read

the omens of us in this market ware
we haven't broken yet but which we will,
the great anonymous! *The very air*

in which they drank left spaces they would fill
with human shape here every night. The glow
of their own sun is in the walls. Distil

me out of that, man, ya?" – Mbulelo,
watching the bubbles lift up through his beer
in gold chains a long way from Soweto

and his shebeens. "But you, however here
and now you are, John, *and* you are, still *you*
know man, you can't, can you, however near

the smell, the very touch of it..." He drew
my ghostly outline in the air. I thought
of Keats drifting through windowpanes, into

the sparrows on a gravel-stoned forecourt,
then of the stuff in Hegel on how bright
the master's soul shines through the slave in wrought-

iron Shakespeare-country chains, then lantern light
and caves and Disney dwarfs singing a hymn
to labour underneath the floor at night,

gems pulsing in their hands, squat sacks a-brim
with jagged treasure glow which they will bear
home on their backs, big headed cherubim,

with mangel-wurzel chins, freaks at the fair,
clowns in Mum's pantomime, knockers down old
dead shafts where draughts still lift their long black hair

and beards, 'Jews', small as ants, whose spells have sold
love's very speech, *my precious, treasure, dear,*
oh heart of gold... "But if you're built on gold,

have gold for ground..." Or have a sepia
gold prospector grandad still posing in
a house in Joburg that he called *Roskear*....

XXVII

It's 1917. He stands there, chin
out, feet set wide apart, and leaning back
as short men do. Grandad Bartle: from tin

Camborne to this, the profile of his black
chauffeur posed at the Studebaker wheel
his wife and children turned to the smart kodak.

Grounds, dining room, library – You feel
the squeal of polish – nursery, parlour
with oil paintings by the younger Cox, real

horns and antelopes' heads, grandfather
himself shirtsleeved at his billiards, cue
in hand, Dutch cartoon showgirl with a garter

on her thigh and great big buckled shoe
behind him in a frame. The tennis court,
the lion rug desperately snarling through

the doorway with its stretched out claws. The wrought
iron beds and walnut desk. He died of drink,
and there were debts. The hotels he had bought

were sold, their home, the rich-girl's mink
he gave her for New York (he'd domineer
and spoil by turns). Her voice was that last link.

"Sing to me." And outside the window near
his deathbed she went through *Abide with Me*
again and yet again possessed by fear

of him even in death till somebody
bent to her ear and told her she could stop.
The chapel solos end and ungodly

sentimental concert party slop
comes from her varnished lips and smile and bare
white shoulders, each earring a rocking drop

of Joburg gold. She turns to lit-up air
inside the darkened rows of eyes that look
out of one single stare, which is his stare.

And hers, and mine. And in a snap they took
of him at infant school, my son Tristan
looks out of it as well, holding a book

next to a classroom globe as if there's one
mask of a face we look out of and make
a world. In him my eyes are African.

XXVIII

It's almost three a.m. Afi's awake
going past the door, downstairs. A light switch snaps.
The windowframe across the grass. The shake

and jingle of the fridge. We've left. The gaps
in what I write are solid. Soft bumps on
the stair carpet, her bare feet, her bra-straps

above her wrapper like a woman from
the village still when she comes in to take
off Lara to her bed. We've left. We've gone.

Pounded yam and peppered stewing steak
for dinner. Hausa on the phone. A store
that sells Gulder. Nights of both being awake.

XXIX

We came because of Mum. Now Dad. One more
year, two maybe, the doctor says he'll live,
shouting at night, repeating psalms, not sure

what day it is, what time, which house. Elusive
as it is, maybe love's what at last
you just admit, what's just the narrative

of who you are: him, or lack of him, a past
as such, it has to seem, made endlessly
of leaving people, being left, a cast

of railway station extras. Old man, wave me
off from that platform one last brave faced time
as window replaces window perfectly.

The summer hols are over, so's the shine
along a breaker, so's Dreamland, the pier,
The Wintergardens' queue that's now a line

shuffling towards a different barrier
and there a woman takes my passport gaze
into her own. I'm going to Zaria,

my city of pale orange walls and haze
at dawn, coconut scented dust, a kite
on motionlessly spread out wings that sways

and flickers its tail feathers at first light
above the market tables and the cones
of yam flour, rice and gari, that far off sight

enlarging everything, the white flagstones
outside where I lived once, the mango tree
that used to clank the roof in rain storms, home's

elusive address still, as now at three
a.m., a drowning voice beneath the floor
boards calls: "Help me! Somebody! Somebody!"

XXX

The cell with walls of bone without a door,
the ceiling with the stars stuck over it,
the manikin who can infer, no more,

the Earth, its things and people from the kit
God's left with him to sift the evidence,
the Brit empiricist imperial bit,

in which the world's nothing but interference
coming very subtly through the tips
of nerves, the way a pianist's audience

in rows of dark, each with just parted lips
and empty eyes, can feel the pianist's touch....
And so on, with a metaphor that grips

us, me, still, yes, I know, however much
I tell myself how many souls there are
to anyone, and see him with his crutch,

that beggar singing Arabic, those far
away ball-bearing eyes, that now once more
implore the empty front seat of my car.

XXXI

And brings me back to my own metaphor –
of primal arms and legs and brain and spine –
which has no time but me beyond the store

of speech balloons it blows, what Wittgenstein
called the best picture of the human soul
as such, and William Blake thought was divine,

a stickman on a rock, part for a whole.
Yes, count the fingers up to ten once more
and say the name you later stole

as *me*. "Somebody" comes up through the floor
again among the show programmes, the rows of
sheet music, my poster on the door

a smiling Fulani girl who shows off
snake-skin bags at some airport boutique
I push past to get his wet bed clothes off.

XXXII

Ayo wrote: "Old infantile hide and seek
leftism! Say *seed*. Say *borehole*. Say *drought*.
These days you'd get deported in a week.

Or less. Or worse. Look at the campus: lockout
demo, shootings. You name it. Just forget
about this place, man. Just forget about

it, John. For lectures now they have to set
up chairs outside and listen through the window.
And to what? Who to? Who will they get

now all the good people have long ago
fled to The States where they can work? We lack
Nelson Mandelas, that's for sure. There's no

point, now, not even if they'd have you back,
which they won't. No money. Economics.
You know how much it cost now for a sack

of rice? Talk about praxis, semiotics,
drive your Beetle, fly home on your free
ticket. See Musa in Finance. He'll fix

you up. Stamp here. Thank you. Your family,
they'll eat meat every day. They'll get their new
clothes, their school books, their toys, tv,

tapes, climb trees and pick mangoes, and you
with beer and laptop on the porch at home
that house built by the Brits in '32

when they first came, using the local stone –
ingenious as ever, let's be fair..."
Or drive to market to pick out a comb

like this one Lara uses for her hair
now lying by her homework on my rug,
pictures of local Fishbourne Palace where

she went on a school trip, where men had dug
and found the ur-imperial way of life:
rubbish pits, dolphin tiles, bones, bits of jug

and vase, Compradorius and his wife
with huge Latino eyes gazing ahead,
the jewels in the handle of a knife.

XXXIII

The rearview mirror frames that beggar's red-
eyed gaze in which I am made rich indeed.
As in a negative, there's black instead

of pallor, white for shadow. Bead by bead
he blesses me, my family, my race –
"Long life, long life," – according to his need.

XXXIV

Rain wrinkling a billboard with my face
nailed on it. Gradually the features lose
shape leaving WANTED in vast upper case.

XXXV

Too high to see, the plane is just an ooze
of white across the downstairs sky Dad's face
is frozen in, watching its wake diffuse

and hang there like a photographic trace
flashed on a textbook page to show the way
time's measured in the separating space

between our molecules. His breakfast tray
appears when he looks down, his Weetabix,
his marmalade. "What day is it today?

Whose house is this?" Yours, Dad, mortar and bricks.
The black-creased AA map of memory
is out of date. Same sky, same wisps and flicks

of torn off cotton wool. Beyond the PT
store room glass, the Spitfires corkscrew wing
tip over wingtip shrinking into Dinky

Toys, then nothing but a sky writing
that ruffles out across the stratosphere.

Inside his Empire of Imagining

what's near is far off and what's far is near,
and names of places alter till they sound
as English as the spire-top cock sings clear,

whatever chants the natives wail around
their fire, over their calabash of wine,
or in some bar in some mud-walled compound

where I, too, glance up at that oozing line
that thins and hangs like crumpled lace. *What date
is it? What time is it? Is this house mine?*

XXXVI

Soon now the muezzin will cry, the crate
of jingling empties crash onto its stack.
This is research as well. Here's how the state

inscribes the morning air and arms and back-
bone, with that *absolute implicitness*
of yours – that Dauda copies from the black-

board, the Emir's red nephew in his rimless
insect-like specs and icing sugar lace
and hula, and still can't spell. *The pencil hisses*

loudest when it's closest to the face,
they say. *The goat jeers from his rubbish mound.*
The Boeing 747 draws out its trace

of white pollution too far from the ground
to have a shape beyond the trail of one,
or to emit the faintest screaming sound

above the clinks of bottles, glasses, sun
on Fairy Liquid rainbowing a plate.
What could you do? What else was to be done

but give up trying to build the juster state
in rich men's children's heads? Except the True
and Faithful aren't so easy to placate.

You're still their stranger and your term's still due.
The churches tumble down. The beer is tipped
into the street. The slogans all come true.

Or so I fear, and see the stand pipes ripped
askew, the rubble walls smoothing already
with the rain, the wrecked car's wheel hubs gripped

still by the road, being drummed into a steady
haze of glittering. A small beam flicks
our random moments on a wall, the ready

smile, lips saying silent words, a wick's
blur inside hurricane lamp glass, neem tree,
table, cement floor, door blind, well, mud bricks,

an *absolute implicitness,* maybe,
along the arms and shoulder blades that know
the weight of things, now, yes speechlessly –

Are you still there? – along the undertow
and heartbeat in the very marks for words,
so it's alleged? That rich, rich, rich cargo.

XXXVII

I'm listening to the tape-recorded birds
that used to filter through my skull an hour
or so before dawn comes when what is heard's

also a sky printed with twigs, moonflower
scent, the banana's tattered silhouette
clearing as through developer, now shower

sounds that aren't rainfall, just the cassette
I once propped in a tree to trap this past
before it came. What is it I regret?

Not just some birds, not just some shadows cast
by lamps across a bar, but the demise,
the whole mess, the whole loss, the whole damned last

coming act that I can visualise
in tv colour close-up. Just how far's
the lens from the dead faces and the flies,

the warlords with their flags on armoured cars
machine gun up, and petrol canister
jammed in the back? Or from those seminars

at which sometimes there'd be that visitor
who'd sit in with his jeans and tie-dye on
and too sharp-cornered pad, and who would later

be there in the bar with fresh-faced bon-
hommie, and microphone inside his vest.
And those trapped souls of ours unravelled on

his spools elsewhere in secret with the best
fidelity the SSS could get.
Our voices started stopped stammered digressed

with not the faintest noise on the cassette.
This was stability. And oil. And Shell
(Nigeria), nine billion dollars nett

per annum, maize fields with a toxic smell,
The Kill and Go's dawn raid, the bayonet,
the letter bomb, the sound proof torture cell....

Midnight lists of things I'm too far from
except to know, seem like a map they drew
their lines across to pacify. Shalom,

Salaam. *What is it that the West can do?* –
But keep the nightmares at the frontiers
undreamed, the poetry from being true.

XXXVIII

The little manikin. Now he appears
from far inland, the frailest tickling speck
of him, coming, already mirror tears

standing before his head, hair to his neck
like grass, the club, the short legs rhythmically
jerking the sky, the lips apart. No check

on this. His height has doubled suddenly,
doubles again, is huge, is now, oh groan
my sky-blue eyelided one, oh slowly

breaking open mist, sweet oils, and drone-
ing table fan, net white as cuckoo-spit
belling, dropping back, belling, blown and blown.

What is it to meet someone? What is it
to see the huge real eyes of them? To bawl
out of each others' baby brains and quit

all sense of who gazes and who's seen, all
hissing skin and hissing hands that slow,
slow, slow away to breath, to air, landfall

at last, to gratitude like amazed wracked Crusoe
beached on the high expanses of that far
off bed. These thoughts like vapour, and a glow

of first light along tall brass posts, the bar
beyond, a door cloth blowing, the still tears
of being there more truly than you are.

XXXIX

I love, thou lovest, he loveth. The spheres
turned on the conjugation of *amo,*
amas, amat. I am, thou art. The tears

of things were simply in their being so.
"I shall have loved!" I hissed towards the stars
beyond the iron grid of that dorm window,

"Thou wilt have loved..." scared that I wouldn't pass
old Bully Shaw's test on the pluperfect,
(in fact just scared stiff of the ruling class).

"He/she/it..." Sentences with no object –
like a schoolboy's desire. Yvonne de Carlo's
paper thighs and squirts of sperm. Subject

and verb, then start again, on through the rows
and columns of who loves and in what time
except tense isn't time and present goes

on locked inside the timeless paradigm
untouchably. And yet the latinate
vocal did touch, each penis jerking line

the finger ran along. *I copulate,*
thou masturbatest. Long words glossing *fart*
and *piss* and *fuck,* and *kiss* as *osculate*

(I thought of lipstick). Latin learned by heart,
like love, "a doing word," says Bully Shaw
and next to me Joe Hansley's shoulders start

up like a two-stroke, face red and stiff jaw
shuddering like constipation fit
to split arsehole from soul – "It seems from your,

shall I say mirth, Hansley, that I've more wit
than I had thought I had!" The palms spread wide
in priestly puzzlement. The brows unknit

and arch, a bulge-eyed sigh, and then the stride,
the shouting yellow teeth, and forelock wildly
flopping, Hansley yanked by the tie. "Outside!

Get out you little savage!" Gradually
edge of palm pushing forelock back in place,
and smoothing pat-pat pat-pat carefully

before our utter silent eyes. The face
comes back to that same ordinary white
that once made Africans think us a race

of ghosts out of the sea and the sun's light
shone orange through the gristle of his ears.
Great men who got the conjugations right

for no reason but snob school pupil's fears
of punishment before us, shield on breast,
the brag: *Ad Sequere*. The driver steers

around the steep slow corner where youths dressed
in jerkins and balaclavas shout up at the glass
we're safe behind, with dubbined boots, with pressed

jerseys. "Savages!" Joe yells, "Barbar-arse
estis!" Or in the cuttings that they send
me from the archive, *vandals, underclass*.

They razed the place. I see the long flames bend
up from the windows, dancing shadows, cheers
and beer cans being chucked. A Roman end.

XL

The chimpanzee skin had been there for years,
before JD had it dry-cleaned, a zip
put in the back, some stiffening in the ears,

and took the glass eyes out so he could slip
his own head grinning in the chimp's and see
the world out of its head. And take a trip

as dark was falling into Sabon Gari
where the queue outside the cinema
scattered when he drew up and casually

leaned a hairy elbow from the car
window to check the times. And when he tried
to make a pickup near a red light bar

waggling a black nailed finger, smiling wide
with all his lovely teeth, his other palm
clumped like a sunhat on his head, the dyed

and beautiful ran screaming. A fire alarm
began. An anthropology professor
from SOAS never would forget the calm

eyes of a chimp framed in his rear-view mirror
as he slowed to turn into the flats,
and how it courteously applied its dimmer....

"Not like Nigerian drivers, feller, that's
for sure," JD said when he'd told the tale.
Those were the pastoral sixties when expats

still ran things, clerks stayed at their desks, no sale
of leaked exam papers, no caving in
to so-called radicals, no stealing mail.

A fairy story, so it seemed to him,
complete with tricks and supernatural fears
of beasts that hide inside a different skin.

XLI

"Your Royal Highness, Foreign Secretary, peers,
industrial magnates, chiefs of staff, scholars –
geographers" [laughter]. The chandeliers

are shining from his cheeks. All Africa's
been shaved away and shrinks into a screen
to point to with a cane. Those travellers,

for all their narratives, what had they *seen?*
"Those Arabs, Romans, men in plumes and hose
who composed sonnets to a black toothed queen –

[laughter again], or drew a man with nose
and mouth and eyes embedded in his chest –
more heart than head, perhaps, you might suppose..."

[laughter, laughter]. The facts are manifest.
The traces of his tracks, the exact ground
to which the very dotted lines attest,

the name he gave a river that he *found,*
the native words for beasts, chiefs, tribes, ranks, cities –
all transcribed, exotic sound by sound.

Incontrovertible transparencies
show everything. Applause, applause, it comes
like rain in front of rain falling through trees.

The calabash tips to his shuddering gums
again. Her forearms gleam. Bird and gecko
burnt into the wood between her thumbs.

Perfect stereotypes. Above, below,
day in day out. A box contains the soul.
It's decorated with cowries. Although

it's yours nothing of you's in it. A scroll
of papers, dates, places, the map and line
like tangled cotton that has neither goal

nor starting point left in it now, nor time.
It must be sent back to the place it came
from, wrapped in waterproof. Her forearms shine.

Mud wall. Mats. Doorframe. Rain in front of rain.
A timeless knock of chalk on blackboard. Wall,
map, the coloured rags of nations. (Again

she tilts the calabash.) A shelf with small
black globes on it and not a frontier
or coast or sea marked over them at all,

only the curving windowpanes. "Don't fear –"
his mother's dying words – "I won't forget you!"
Not in this loop and tangle ending here.

What is now? Mud wall, doorway, face, "Bless you!"
in English. Cloth. Face. Wall. Doorway. Face. Face.
"There was no far source I wanted to get to!"

XLII

Exotic trophies in the market place,
the muddy Aztec spud, cotton as near
as skin, the cupsa char – *shayi* – that trace

your fortune backwards to its dregs, the here
and now of orange juice and bedtime cocoa,
bedtime story where the quay-sides cheer

and Jim and those plantation owners go,
plump cheeked and middle aged, towards the dune
marked *x* in red ink like a kiss, below

which treasure lies.... As homely as a tune
with imitation tom-toms in the beat,
and Dad's hands on the keys. Under its moon,

under its stage-set sun, with steel-tipped feet
Uncle Ernie dances (straw hat, blacked face)
and Mum sings lyrics I can still repeat

and repeat in my head across that space
of dark, mouthing the words with her on stage,
closer than any possible embrace.

XLIII

The face flat in the paper, we engage
with that, the human body as a trace
of light left by an instant flash, from page

three's breakfast table boobs in paper space
and paper time (and *sitting pretty* there)
to that man as exact in date and place –

6th August '44 – changed by a glare
of light into his shadow on a wall
as swimsuited Enola Gay kicked bare

long legs and waved back at the writhing ball
of ash. The shape's perfect but can alas
"have no pretension to being what we'd call

human but their exterior form", Long's crass
History says. Mere shadows, mere scare-quotes
of men, God's similes plus biomass.

Beyond the bookshop glass the slave ship floats
towards the buyer, breasty figurehead
and flag and dreaming sails as if the throats

below the waterline exhaled, instead
of groans, close hymnbook harmonies and blues.
A cultural heritage, a living dead.

Their songs top all the charts. They make us lose
all sense of time and place. And dance. And buy.
Since history's our market and we choose.

XLIV

Oh love, oh love, oh love, oh love, they cry
into their microphones. Its festival
fills up the world from muddy grass to sky.

Love is a sound. It's huge. It's portable.
Its crash tink-tink thub in a Panasonic
headset makes the street inaudible

a heart-thud out of heart-shaped unmelodic
unromantic and unsolitary
Africa. Its primal electronic

fire dissolves the sweatshop circuitry
that holds the globe. As if a single throat
could own its lies, its truth, its honesty,

as if there were this placid silver moat
encircling the sense of self and place
and who we are's not really as remote

as any algebra of time and space,
or third world factory making the shiny
surfaces on which I leave my trace

of utter individuality
in whorls that I can zoom to analyse
(the spyglass icon) indubitably,

and not just fingerprints, either, but eyes,
eyes and their love as well. They too will show
up in the chemistry of that device

that when I gaze into its gaze will know
and find me out, *Ping* like a barcode scan,
black row upon black row upon black row.

XLV

Malam Deaf-and-Dumb-Man, Malam *Ban
da harsa,* Malam No-One-Makes-a-Clown
Malam Noises, Malam Nameless-Man.

Malam Not-Even-A-Word, a pronoun,
even, even *You,* you who sit beside
me in the bar, you with your chatty frown

and smile, my close associate, who'll guide
a palm across the air for me to splash
Oh Mr Shaking-Hands-and-Smiling-Wide

and-Smiling, and with your tie-pin on, and brash
throat noises trying to make the noises mean
the simple civil things like *Hello. Dash*

me Star, but which they never can, they've been
much too long colonised already, from
however deep down in your throat they seem

to come, can't be sincere and can't belong
to you, your jagged bubbles full of ARGHHH!
across the silent pages of King Kong

Monster Comic, Tarzan – Caliban...
And here's the nameless outer inner curse
you've never heard, you Anti-Superman,

Slave Boy strong as Mr Universe
who bellows out his paper agony
like primal self-expression in a verse....

The drinkers jerk their chins up at him very
courteously with, "Hi, red arse'd baboon!
And how your mamma, now? How her wet fanny?"

Reggae comes up through your sandals, and soon –
since without hearing what they'd said you know
and turn away and dance – the beat and tune

fill up your shins and thighs, and every hollow
of your bones. And it's the skeleton they say
that knows best how to dance, the skull and no

one else that truly hears the beat, and may-
be yes somewhere there could exist that other
island dialect somehow in the way

the bark, squiggling ponds might somehow utter
some reply. How many years is it
since you've been shouting to me, Malam Mummer

with your eyebrows lifted and the lit
up wrinkles piling up your forehead to
the hair, to fix me here, articulate

in mouthing big. A *Star?* I point to you
and then the bottle by me. Single shake
of head. Then: *Double Crown?* Another cue.

Now single nod. I can't help it. I make
the mouths although he can't lip-read, of course.
And then as happens sometimes when you take

somebody's eyes a moment into yours
and you're remembering together all
the other times, I go back to those roars

I heard first standing at the suya stall
across the street, through pepper smoky air
above the charcoal flames, and through your wall.

And through walls and through walls as if somewhere
the eyelids of a child, me as a boy
perhaps, flicked open in the dark aware

not just of windowframe, clock, mirror, toy
Messerschmitt, but heard, as he still can,
the terrifying sounds of human joy.

XLVI

Autistic were they, Tarzan, Peter Pan,
Mowgli, those hunters through our videos
and comic strips – Tammylan, Caliban,

Green Man, who come back and come back like those
ghost abikus, "half savage and half child"
in Kipling's words that might just be Rousseau's?

Emile, I thought of, sitting in the *Wild
Zone* fenced off in Lara's primary school.
Thistles, foxgloves, tussocks. They looked exiled

in very abandonment next to the rule
and grid left by the mower. Stones to sit
on to watch dragonflies, and weeds like gruel

below a surface suede. The last of it,
this way of learning, where the net's brought
dribbling up with mud, and sprigs and grit

and something silver's wriggling like the thought
of it drawn into light (And out of no
ring-binder telling England what it ought

to learn and when and at what level) though
the nymph just drawn out of its element
was suffocating slowly in the shadow

of the scientific faces bent
to it exploring their discovery,
and writhing please oh God just to be sent

into its ignorance, again. *Go free,*
we say, half-thinking without thinking, what
it might be like inside another body

and yet still ourselves, which is the lot
and every character in every story,
isn't it? – including what I jot

down among dragonflies in this diary
for Laraba to read, the numbered days
of memory before her memory

can be, yes, captured, from me and my ways
of loving her... rambling like this, – in black-
berry fields, puffballs floating, and grass sways

against the sky, now dimming streets, door-clack,
a jar and fish on string like lantern light
glinting the unlit glass. "Mum! Mum! I'm back!"

XLVII

I dreamt of coming – going – back last night,
the train gloonking and glinking slowly over
shiny rail towards some early flight,

the shadow of a toothbrush and a beaker
on frosted glass, and then the fields, a lake
of silver sky, seagulls behind a tractor,

furrows as damp and black as christmas cake,
the girl taking my heavy bag from me
matching the face I can't see with the fake

one staring from the page, and now the key
floats at my thighbone, those last coins I need
no longer and no longer currency,

and things known always – cars, walls, trees, bindweed,
clouds – now through a small window these
all rush towards me at tremendous speed.

XLVIII

Another dream: Ayo under the trees
sprawled barefoot on the front seat of his taxi
reading *South,* the stereo on, his keys

with Che's head dangling from them. HISTORY,
he's had somebody paint for him, STILL RIDES
WITH US. But not in the academy.

In the same letters on the other side's
ALLUTA, nothing else. "Our classroom farce's,
over, man, he grins." The Datsun slither-slides

through motor park mud and puddles, passes
meat hawkers, holdalls, touts calling. We come
to gates and now the road. Slouch hat, dark glasses

flower shirt, he guns the engine; thrum
turns ragged fart; dust fills the rearview; tink
of winkers, bare foot right down. Now we've swum

out wide to overtake, but no, flash blink-
blinking headlamps and a tanker's iron wall
rises in front of us. Okay, we jink

back in, fast whirls of steering wheel, all
easy elbows, though, then right at our brake
lights suddenly another caterwaul

of parp and parp. Amazingly we make
it and slide out again, out into emptied
pure blue road just waiting there to take

us in, and clicking Fela on to plead
his "Follow follow follow," Ayo goes
for it, up to his bare shin-bone in speed.

XLIX

Outside, the almost coming first light shows
things as the shadows of themselves before
colour, thickness and English names enclose

their shapeless ghosts inside their shapes once more.
No word for it, except the glossary
of Sweet's *Old English Reader,* has this word-store

word for what seems now a more third worldly
kind of time, the-hour-before-dawn: *uhta.*
That guy a thousand years ago, maybe,

gone schizoid with remorse, or just a hearer
of voices, was voices, still is, still rows
across his moody ocean. *Anhaga,*

somebody who's hedged in, who also knows
how not being dead when others are, is to:
"experience the curving sky one goes

towards as one's own curving skull." "Untrue!
Untrue!" they shout, "No belly-aching yet
ever changed any coward's Fate." On cue

they float in rippling mail on the sea fret
towards him as he's screaming their names straight
into their faces, as he blubbers: "Let

me just explain!" and they disintegrate
into the almost coming dawn. A con.
A sentence from Boethius on Fate.

"And you dream. That the Führer's hand rests on
your hair again. You're his, you're his, you swear.
Then wake remembering high stone walls gone

to ruin, the work of giants, standing there
abandoned completely. You watch the breeze
blow dust like your own breath into that air.

Here Fate finished them off as if to please
the need for closure in a narrative
and leave nothing. Except some elegy's

hit and miss flights from lip and to lip, some native
pagan lay altered to make it flow
out of the quill of some monk trying to give

some soul a Christian course he couldn't know
was there. Download it. There's the parchment, stains
and all. *Anhaga: hedged around,* and so

enclosed – caught in the bone cell of the brains.
An which is one, and *haga:* hedge, akin
to hawthorn, hodge, Hodges, Hay, Hayward, Haynes,

that ghost in the machine nobody's in,
that Haynes the Englishman, his aspirate,
his diphthong, his nasal, his final thin

voiced sibilant, his lips and tongue estate,
his squirl of ink, one with the Windies bat
and Fulham wizard, thorn and leaf, the great

house built of sugar, and slavery. *That,*
this, here, there, I, you. Abi, yu deh grin,
Patience. Your feet even in heels are flat.

L

The patchwork fields below him bank and spin
around the stillness of a pilot's aim
reflecting tail-struts, swastikas, a thin

brown pencil line of smoke becoming flame.
The falling scrag of parachute billows,
slows, sways over the hedges that Dad's name,

no matter who he is, goes back to, blows
sideways across a lake like bathroom glass,
grass blurring, steps going up, pillars, windows,

towers, battlements built once by that class
of country gentlefolk whose chained-up souls
wait on the quay at Calabar and Brass

for them although already now the Rolls
crackling the gravel flies an *ardua*
ad astra flag and there are football goals

set on the lawns, and still the erks who clatter
down the steps with Lee Enfields and race
across the green, green as Arcadia

still, have in them – and Dad is one – that space
of well kept wilderness – though not a blade
of it is theirs – from when they learnt to trace

the red rags on the map we don't invade
but civilise where brave pale women teach
native children how true character's made

under a pastoral tree and dark hands reach
upwards to answer about cloth and shame
about virtue and industry and each

one has a special English Christian name,
like yours. Here's the invader now. They run
towards him, this eighteen-year-old who came

down in an unreal field and holds a gun
in fingers that have no skin left and bright
holes in his face instead of eyes. The Hun.

LI

Of course I know it isn't *you* I write
to sitting with elbows each side of a beer
chin in your palms and fingers splaying bright

red nails across your cheeks, you who lean near
and slowly close your eyes and then as slowly
open them so that the doubt goes as clear

through mine as through the very ghost of me.
"All dis tok-tok. Na dis, na dat, na dis...!
John? Enh? Wettin now? Me I no sabi!"

Then closer still, the quick touch of the kiss.
Me I no sabi, although you *do.*
A word or two of Pidgin can dismiss

all mine, can't they? Of course. Because for you
the words, most of them borrowed English though
they are, are mother tongue and come into

the breath across your tongue and lips as no
talk *full of grammah* could. I've watched them split
and writhe on the oscilloscope and know

the alterings. I am a prof of it
forgodsake, language once taught by the whips
and probably, as Bickerton has it,

made up by kids, who mapped the shapes of lips
to kinds of pain and both to forms akin
to gut-known Kwa – marked now with scholarship's

circumspect star: nothing is written in
it. It is hypothetical. The play
of thought over a corpus of, yes, *sin,*

what else? There's nothing I can say.
It's true. The singer sings, the drinkers drink
their bottles empty, stand, and go away.

It's true I too deh tok, I too deh tink.
And yet, look at the photograph. You see
how words grow solid? In a child? And link

all this up into bones and blood and lovely
flesh – all this, yes, crime, from which, no sense
of it, or speaking's, going to set us free.

LII

It's getting light. The ghost next to your fence
fades like a see-through lover back into
his other world and other day's events,

leaving the burglar bars to come on cue
like squares drawn on a map or like those frames
that artists used to use to catch the true

67

appearances of time, and find the planes
and vanishings and angles in the land
whose secret longitude's the eye's and brain's.

My continents of blots turn into bland
back garden posts and trees, and blackbirds *sing*
or so we say as if they understand

this other world and day to which we bring
the patterns of their whistling. The hoopoe
also. I can hear its tink and ting

among cutout leaves outside your window,
jerking its beak the way that thoughts occur
inside a brain. Across the bush the shadow

boy clicks to the cows. Their white flanks blur
with early light. Their sleep-walking horns clatter
and clack together gently as they stir

the orange dust around their hocks and scatter
egrets from under the sharp-edged mango
shade. And closer, Gizo-gizo, patter

man and trickster, spins the alter ego
we have made out of the silk inside
him for the folk tales that he doesn't know

for all the changing shapes he has defied
the powerful with, swinging on his own gleam
of gossamer. Its half-arcs wink and slide

about under my hedge. The coffee cream
is spiralling. The letter-box-springs whack.
I'm kneeling to my mail. The fur-like steam

is on my cheek. Then upstairs, past the crack
of open door, Lara sleeping in bed
and Toad's eyes glaring from the pillow. Back

in here, the screen of flying stars, the head
that John Saungueme brought from Zambia
that time *i-smuggled through customs,* he said.

Bark beard, receding hair. Might almost be a
bust of him, that shining Lenin brow.
He floats up from the wood. He's here. You're here.

No need of any clearance stamp with *now*
banged in in present tense. I press, have pressed
the keys as though just typing will endow

the air with listening. Since you're addressed
you must be *there,* just as the dawn birds *sing,*
or someone's *in* our heads, or the dead *rest,*

or what I write, what I'm not finishing,
however I address it's going to *find*
you. As we say. Bilkisu rang. She'll bring

this on the plane. She'll stand at that door-blind,
flipflops and varnished toe-nails through the sand,
calling "Pam-pam? Pam-pam?" next to the lined

up crates. There, inside: shadowy, a fan
whirring over empty tables, and less
clear, further in, a pail? A dustpan...?

Love, I've got to get up now and dress.

NOTES

Canto I

P11 *a single now:* Nigeria and Britain fall along the same longitude and, during British summer time, have the same clock time.

Canto IV

P15 *Pythagoras:* Pythagoras is thought to have visited and brought mathematical ideas from Arabia and possibly further east.

Canto V

P15 *nyash:* Pidgin: bum.

P16 *esewu:* Calabar dish made with chopped goat head and spiced sauce.

P16 *Fine-fine na...:* Pidgin. You'll make books very well, John, with this kind of brain inside you.

Canto VII

P18 *where Tarzan used to come to see his cache:* Tarzan, the hero of Edgar Rice Burroughs' novels, was born in the West African rain forest, after his parents had been set adrift in a mutiny. In *Tarzan of the Apes*, his father builds a cabin which, after his parents are dead, Tarzan stumbles upon not knowing it had been his birthplace. He finds books, some of them children's books intended for him, from which he miraculously teaches himself to read, but not speak, English. He calls the printed letters 'bugs'.

Canto X

P20 *to people with desire:* The idea that the early colonists thought of the places they 'discovered' as empty of people, *carte blanche* for the imagination, comes from Octabe Mannoni in *Prospero and Caliban: The Psychology of Colonization* (Ann Arbor, 1996).

P21 *some barque of Injun gold was guided by:* The barque is often used as an image in Petrarch's love poetry, which so affected poets like Walter Ralegh who was at least figuratively guided in his actual voyages by his attachment to Queen Elizabeth whom he usually speaks of as Diana or Cynthia and in the third person but occasionally he substitutes the more intimate second person. The gold which he and others went to the New World to bring back for the Queen was, of course, the property of the Native Americans.

Canto XI

P21 *tyre boys:* Punctures are mended by vulcanisors who have simple roadside lean-tos built out of scrap material. Often a ten or twelve year old will fan the naked flame to melt the rubber which will plug the puncture.

P22 *Na you don mek di blod....:* It's you who made the blood I sing with red.

Canto XII

P23 *'Life's but a wayside farm'*: From the Ewe oral poet Akpalu, translated by Kofi Awoonor.

P23 *Sunday*: Clerk in Letter Writer's office. Not from Hanwa village like most of the team. Sunday is a Christian name.

P23 *Sani*: Northern radical academic of aristocratic background, favouring a Black Stalin revolution in Nigeria.

P23 *Saddam*: Most Nigerians saw the Gulf War from an anti-Western perspective, and in the North it was seen as anti-muslim.

P23 *CIA*: The CIA is seen as a terrorist organisation, the World Bank as a tool of the privileged business interests in these Third World countries, run by so-called 'compradors'.

P23 *so-called Marxist expatriates*: Among Nigerian Marxists, so-called Western Marxism is seen as over intellectualised 'revisionism' which over-emphasises democracy and consciousness.

P24 *quill of creosote*: The tables in Patience's Parlour are made of planks protected with creosote but sometimes spikes of wood, hardened by the creosote, stick up or out like quills.

Canto XIII

P24 *fetish*: Could be a passage from the Koran folded into a pendant, sometimes the water in which the words have been 'washed off' the page.

P24 *Mission Scholars*: Samaru and other Northern townships like it were originally built by the British. They needed local clerks and other staff and these had to know English, which Northern Nigerians did not. Southern Nigerians were brought into northern areas as Christian 'allies' of the British, and this sowed the seeds of later inter religious and inter ethnic conflicts.

P24 *Mandate*: Frederick Lugard's *Dual Mandate* set out his ideas for the relationship between colonisers and colonised in Africa.

P25 *almajarai*: Boys, who study The Koran with a Malam and beg alms for him.

P25 *dim Mercedes Benz*: Most of the time different ethnic groups live together peacefully in Northern Nigeria. Conflicts are almost always fomented by 'big men' whose status is shown by their ownership of the talismanic Mercedes. Such 'alhajis' frequently supplied and organised apparently spontaneous riots, which could be very violent and bloody indeed, as was shown in the 1992 conflict in nearby town of Kaduna. In 1967-8 rioting and wholesale killing provoked in Kano, Zaria and other Northern cities by the assassination of the then Head of State, Tafawa Balewa, and the Sardauna, leader of Northerners, by young Igbo officers led to the cessation of the then Eastern (Igbo) Region of Nigeria (which took the name of Biafra) and then to the Nigerian Civil War.

71

Canto XVI

P27 *Laraba:* Hausa girl's name meaning 'Wednesday' after the day of birth. Shortened to Lare or here 'anglicised' to Lara.

P28 *Czar...Come on and Hear:* The Czar referred to is Czar Alexander, who was made the 'Alexander' of *Alexander's Rag Time Band* by Irving Berlin, from which THE BESTEST BAND THAT AM is a quotation.

P28 *Tin Pan Alley pioneers:* The most prominent makers of Hollywood style 'America' and modern popular music were descended from Jewish immigrants fleeing from oppression in Europe. Irving Berlin, George Gershwin, Jerome Kern also all drew upon Black jazz, and both Kern and Gershwin made musical plays with Black characters in them, (Cole Porter, though he drew on African music and experience of North Africa, was, of course, not a Jew,) and seem to have identified – as far as a *That's Entertainment* ideology would allow – with the Blacks in America.

P29 *Julie's song of common love... Mum's (or Ava Gardner's) skin*: In the film of *Show Boat* the racially mixed character, Julie, played by Ava Gardner (who is not of mixed race) is dismissed from the show because of her 'blood'. The song of common love is *Bill*, by Jerome Kern and P G Wodehouse. In the film of *Show Boat* Ava Gardner singing is in fact dubbed, but not in the related CD.

P29 *Fats:* Fats Waller, born Thomas Wright Waller, African American jazz pianist (1904-44), a strong influence on the Letter Writer's father's piano playing.

Canto XVII

P29 *Vatsa:* Major General and poet, Mamman Vatsa, was third in seniority in the military junta led by General Ibrahim Babangida, who had Vatsa executed by firing squad in March 1986 as an alleged coup plotter.

P29 *national scars:* Traditional scars made on the cheeks which often identify people by ethnic/local group.

P29 *RASTA:* Rhymes with previous 'mastah' but not fully with Vatsa. However, 'Vasta' is often pronounced 'Vassa', and 'mastah' 'massah'.

P29 *Star(s)*: a type of lager.

P29 *great city:* Abuja, the new Federal Capital, the building of which Mamman Vatsa was administering, a task which he invested a great deal himself in, and also planned a Russian style Writers' Village, which has, well after the time this poem is set, and after several hiccups, finally been completed.

P30 *Shell Nigeria:* The Shell Oil Company has huge influence over the oil-based economy of post-colonial Nigeria.

P30 *shot:* On 25 February, 1986 Vatsa was found guilty with ten other officers of plotting a coup against Babangida. The execution took placed publicly by firing squad on Bar Beach, Lagos on 5 March, 1986. There is doubt as to whether Vatsa and others were in fact plotting a coup.

P30 *ANA:* Association of Nigerian Authors. During this conference Vatsa acted as tour guide to members who went round in a coach to see the then very far from completed Federal Capital. He was on the committee of the Association and helped it with funds.

P30 *The Casino Afro:* Nigerian radicals see financial arrangements in relation to the West, especially by Nigeria 'compradors' and/or the World Bank, in terms of gambling and gamblers, forbidden by Islam.

Canto XVIII

P31 *madman:* Not an altogether uncommon sight in Nigerian cities. The brolly and suit and sometimes the bowler or top hat are throw-backs to colonial times and are still used ceremonially in some areas, for example of Calabar, to signify status and power.

P31 *bori:* traditional pre-Islamic spirit.

Canto XIX

P31 *Calabar:* Calabar is associated with the earliest exploitation of West Africa in the slave trade.

Canto XX

P32 *I keep seeing that blackened car...:* The events described are based on aspects of the last chapter of Nadine Gordimer's novel, *A Guest of Honour* when Becky, having survived the attack in which her lover, Bray, had been killed, flies to England.

P33 *dung beetle's spit:* In an earlier part of the novel Bray had contemplated his own life as a timeless whole. "He was returned to himself, neither young nor middle-age, neither secreting the spit of individual consciousness nor using it to paste together the mud-nest of an enclosing mode of life." *A Guest of Honour,* (Penguin, 1970), p231.

Canto XXI

P33 *The Whiteman's soul is black:* An ANC and Black Consciousness slogan.

P33 *abiku:* in Yoruba mythology a child which dies soon after birth and then returns as the next child to be born of the same mother.

P34 *'Mistah John – he black':* *The Heart of Darkness* (Penguin, 1994), p37.

P34 *Mbulelo:* Mbulelo Mzamane, South African novelist and critic, that time ANC refugee, who worked with Steve Biko. His novel, *The Children of Soweto*, (Longman, 1982) provides a diary of the schoolchildren's rising of 1976.

P34 *African time:* A phrase used originally by expatriates to mock the lack of punctuality of West Africans but in fact marking different conceptions of time.

Canto XXII

P34 *A myth:* The figure is like the idealised former Mau Mau guerrilla in Ngugi wa 'Thiongo's popular novel, *Matigani* (Heinemann, 1987), and Paolo Friere whose literacy through consciousness raising in the villagers was faintly echoed by the Letter Writer's work when in Nigeria.

P35 *Gizo-gizo*: Hausa: 'Spider', trickster figure in traditional fables

Canto XXIII

P35 *An endless sense of love:* A quote from Che Guevara on the qualities needed in a revolutionary.

P35 *manjar janar:* Hausa form of 'major general'.

Canto XXIV

P36 *It's us and London Scottish:* Rugby is played by teams in the main cities of Nigeria. Although begun by the British, now, most of the players are Nigerian, and a majority of the Zaria team were farmers from the small village of Hanwa.

P36 *Zazzau:* Zaria as emirate, administrative area.

Canto XXV

P37 *horses... turbans... spears... drums:* The Durbah is another ritual, held on the same field as the Zaria rugby team plays on. The Durbah is an example of the 'invention of tradition'."The most far-reaching inventions of tradition in colonial Africa took place when the Europeans believed themselves to be respecting age-old African custom. What were called customary law, customary land-rights, customary political structure and so on, were in fact all invented by colonial codification." (Terrence Ranger:*The Invention of Tradition In Colonial Africa*, Cambridge University Press, 1983).

P37 *Sarki:* The prospective Emir (Sarki) comes first. Traditionally he is the ruler of Zaria.

P37 *Now Sirens:* The military governor arrives second, and is the one to 'appoint' the Emir, as the British had selected (and debarred) candidates.

P37 *Soja Gwabna:* Military governor (of the state).

P37 *the dog, Lugard:* Frederick Lugard, the conqueror and first Governor General of Nigeria, who set up 'indirect rule' whereby the colonial power rules through the Nigerian elite, which in the north were the Fulani ruling families who supplied the emirs. *The Kano Chronicle* (1902) refers to the invading British as dogs: 'these dogs will overcome us!'.

Canto XXVI
P39 *Shakespeare-country chains:* Iron goods used by slave traders, guns and chains particularly, came mainly from the midlands, the 'Black country' as it is called.

P40 *knockers:* Cornish 'little people' said to haunt tin mines, sometimes thought to be the ghosts of dead Jews. They were believed to get smaller each year of their existence till they were the size of ants.

P40 *Roskear:* then a tin mining area of Cornwall.

Canto XXVII
P41 *my eyes are African:* the Letter Writer's children being of mixed race.

Canto XXVIII
P42 *Gulder:* Nigerian brand of lager.

Canto XXXII
P44 *Ayo:* Ayo Ajagun, a former trades union activist, then student of the Letter Writer, then Lecturer in Education, is now a taxi driver.

P44 *deported:* Refers to the Letter Writer's involvement in 'street theatre' and 'conscientization' in Nigerian villages.

P45 *Compradorius:* The 'client king' Tiberius Claudius Cogidubnus. A Briton who took Roman citizenship and acted much like a present day 'comprador'.

Canto XXXVI
P47 *hula:* traditional Muslim peakless cap.

P48 *absolute implicitness:* Patience, in an article called 'The Social Mud', writes of history's *"absolute implicitness in the stone and mud of the everyday past"*.

Canto XXXVII
P49 *SSS:* Nigeria state secret police.

P49 *The Kill and Go's:* paramilitary police.

Canto XL
P53 *JD:* Old school British expatriate who had been in Zaria some thirty years. This was JD's idea of a joke, scaring the superstitious natives.

P53 *expats still ran things:* For some ten years after Nigerian independence in 1960, although the Vice chancellor was a Nigerian, expatriates held most of the key administrative and academic posts.

Canto XLI

P54 *black toothed queen:* Elizabeth I.

P54 *nose and mouth and eyes embedded in his chest:* as described by Sir John Mandeville referring in fact to Native Americans, and taken up in Shakespeare's *Othello*.

P54 *found:* A now stock Afrocentric response to the European idea that explorers *discovered* this or that people is to ask whether these countries and peoples were not there already.

P54 *burnt:* Calabashes used to drinking and other things are often decorated with stylised lizards, birds and other everyday creatures or plants. These are sometimes burnt into the wood.

Canto XLII

P55 *shayi:* Hausa: tea.

P56 *Jim:* Jim Hawkins from *Treasure Island* by Robert Louis Stevenson (Penguin, 1994).

P56 *Uncle Ernie:* son of the great music hall comedian Dan Leno.

P56 *repeat and repeat:* quotation from Cole Porter's song *I've Got You Under My Skin*.

Canto XLIII

P56 *Enola Gay:* Name of the superfortress that dropped the first atom bomb. Her cartoon pin-up was painted on the nose of the plane.

P56 *Long's crass History:* Edward Long: *History of Jamaica* (1774) racist account cited by Brian V Street in *The Savage in Literature* (Routledge and Kegan Paul, 1975).

P57 *history's our market:* Idea taken from *The Condition of Post-modernity* by David Harvey (Blackwell, 1989).

Canto XLV

P58 *Ban da harsa:* Hausa: 'I have no language/tongue'.

P58 *Star, Double Crown:* As P29. Brands of bottled lager.

Canto XLVI

P60 *Autistic:* Despite the myths of Enkidu, (perhaps) Oedipus, Mowgli, Tarzan and others, no feral child has yet learnt to speak a human language, but it has at the same time been impossible to prove that such children weren't autistic or otherwise afflicted before being exposed.

P60 *Tammylan:* wild man in Enid Blyton's *The Children of Cherry Tree Farm* (Country Life, 1940)

P60 *abiku:* as P33.

P60 *this way of learning:* The so-called 'progressive' or child-centred view of education which has links with Rousseau's book, *Emile,* and 'primitivism'.

Canto XLVIII

P63 *Fela*: Fela Ransome Kuti, Nigerian popular musician, and radical, one of whose lyrics, *Mr Follow,* runs " Follow follow follow".

Canto XLIX

P63 *That guy:* Protagonist of the Old English poem, 'The Wanderer'. This canto, like the previous two is a journey poem, and like XLVII invokes a dream. The Old English poem dramatises a transition, in the protagonist, from an authoritarian and militaristic group ethos to solitary Christian contemplation about the purpose of life.

P64 *Haynes:* A surname usually associated with the Enclosures movement as well as having an Anglo-Saxon origin. It derives from the Anglo-Saxon word 'haga' meaning 'hedge' or 'enclosure'. The word 'anhaga' in 'The Wanderer' means 'solitary person', hedged around. There are also Joyce's "Haynes, the Englishman" and Desmond Haynes, the West Indian batsman, Johnny Haynes, former Fulham footballer and England captain.

P65 *Abi yu deh grin:* Pidgin: "you may well grin".

Canto L

P65 *patchwork fields...country gentlefolk:* The traditional patchwork pattern of English fields derives from the Enclosure movement. Enclosures were administered by the gentry. A number of well known country houses and estates were built on the proceeds of the Atlantic slave trade, as is the fictional one in this poem.

P65 *ardua ad astra:* The motto of the RAF. The country house was taken over as an RAF base during the Second World War.

Canto LI

P66 *All dis tok-tok. Na dis, na dat, na dis... John? Enh?:* Pidgin: All this talking, first his, then that, then this. John, eh, what's the matter? I don't understand.

P67 *grammah:* Standard English.

P67 *Bickerton:* Linguist who developed a theory that pidgins were devised by the children of slaves using often common basic structures in their own different languages, with English vocabulary. See Derek Bickerton, *Roots of Languages* (Karoma Publishers, 1981).

P67 *Kwa:* Family of West African languages, which includes Yoruba. Basis of West African Pidgin grammar.

Canto LII

P68 *Gizo-gizo:* As p35, Spider.

P69 *John Saungueme:* Zimbabwian radical in exile in Nigeria at the time.

P69 *Bilkisu:* Bilkisu Labaran, former lecturer/colleague of the Letter Writer at Ahmadu Bello, later BBC World Service producer in London.

P67 *Pam-pam:* Uttered when or instead of knocking on a door.

ACKNOWLEDGEMENTS

Acknowledgements are due to the editors of the following publications in which parts of this poem, some of them reshaped since, have been published: *Ambit, Critical Quarterly, London Magazine, Poetry Review, Poetry Wales, Stand Magazine, Wasafiri, Tying the Song* (Enitharmon, 2000).

Thanks are due also to John Greening, Matthew Sweeney, Thomas Lynch, and Mimi Khalvati for criticism.